STRATEGIC BUSINESS MANAGEMENT

NAVIGATING THE MODERN BUSINESS LANDSCAPE

DR. JAGADEESH PILLAI

|| Dedicated to all wisdom seekers around the world ||

ᐁᐁᐁ

Contents

Contents

Prayer

"Om Bhadram Karnebhih Shrunuyaama
DevaahBhadram Pashyemaakshabhiryajatraah
SthirairangaistushtuvaamsastanoobhihVyashema
Devahitam YadaayuhSwasti Na Indro
VridhashravaahSwasti Nah Pooshaa
VishwavedaahSwasti Nastaarkshyo ArishtanemihSwasti
No Brihaspatir DadhaatuOm Shantih, Shantih, Shantih"

The literal meaning of this mantra is: OM. O Gods! Let us
hear auspicious words from our ears. O reverent Gods! Let
us behold propitious visions from our eyes, let our organs
and body be stable, healthy, and strong. Let us do that
which is pleasing to the gods in the life span allotted to us.
May Indra, inscribed in the scriptures, bring us fortune!
May Pushan, the knower of the world, grant us prosperity!
May Trakshya, who vanquishes enemies, bestow us with
blessings! May Brihaspati bring us success!
OM Peace, Peace, Peace.

ᐰᐰᐰ

About The Author

Dr. Jagadeesh Pillai is a renowned Guinness World Record holder, writer, and researcher hailing from Varanasi, also known as the abode of Lord Shiva. With a Ph.D. in Vedic Science and a range of creative ideas and achievements, he is a true polymath. He is the author of more than 100 books including Research Publications. Although his roots can be traced back to Kerala, the people of Varanasi hold him in high regard and affectionately consider him one of their own.

In 1998, Dr. Pillai was offered a job at Banaras Hindu University, but he left the position after only two months to pursue greater goals in life. He believed that in order to study Indian scriptures and engage in other creative endeavours, he needed to retire from the daily grind of working solely for money at a young age.

He started an export business from scratch, using the knowledge he had gained from a previous job in the industry. His intelligence and unique approach to business led to great success in a short period of time, earning him more in just a decade and a half than he would have in a lifetime working in a government job. Upon the passing of Dr. APJ Abdul Kalam, Dr. Pillai decided to leave the business and dedicate himself to reading, studying, researching, and experimenting.

During his tenure in the export business, Dr. Pillai traveled to over 16 countries, gaining valuable insight and experiencing the world and life in detail.

Dr. Pillai has achieved four Guinness World Records in the following subjects:

"Script to Screen" - In this record, Dr. Pillai produced and directed an animation film within the shortest time possible, breaking the previous record set by Canadians. He has also received numerous national and international awards and recognitions for this achievement.

Longest Line of Postcards - For this record, Dr. Pillai created a line of 16,300 postcards on the occasion of the 163rd anniversary of Indian Postal Day. The event also included a questionnaire about the Indian flag.

Largest Poster Awareness Campaign - Dr. Pillai designed an awareness campaign on the subject of "Beti Bachao - Beti Padhao" (Save the Girl Child - Educate the Girl Child) to achieve this record.

Largest Envelope - In tribute to the Indian Prime Minister's "Make in India" initiative, Dr. Pillai created a 4000 square meter envelope using waste paper to achieve this record.

Attempted - **70000 Candles on a 210 kg Cake** - To celebrate the 70th Indian Independence Day, Dr. Pillai attempted to light 70,000 candles on a 210 kg cake, which was recorded in World Records India.

Attempted - **Documentary on Dhamek Stupa of Sarnath in 17 Languages** - Dr. Pillai attempted to create a documentary on the Dhamek Stupa of Sarnath, dubbing it in 17 different languages. The result of this attempt is currently awaiting confirmation from the Guinness World Records.

Dr. Pillai is skilled in teaching the Bhagavad Gita, a Hindu scripture, and is popular among young people. He has helped many young people improve their lives through his motivational teachings.

In addition to teaching, he has composed and sung numerous Sanskrit Bhajans and patriotic songs.

He has also written and directed several short films and documentaries for awareness campaigns, and has volunteered with the police in both UP and Kerala to spread awareness about various issues through videos and photography.

Incredibly, he has produced and directed over 100 documentaries about the city of Varanasi, all on his own.

He has also helped and guided more than 25 boys and girls to achieve world records through creative and innovative methods. He is a multifaceted person who uses his intellect and the blessings given to him by God to excel in various areas. He is both a teacher and a student, always learning and teaching, and is able to master any subject he comes across.

He is a selfless social activist and motivational speaker who has overcome struggles and failures to become a successful and enthusiastic individual with a rich life experience.

In addition to his work with the Bhagavad Gita, he is also an efficient Tarot card reader, Astro-Vastu consultant, and a talented singer and composer. He has sung the entire Ram Charita Manas and Bhagavad Gita in his own compositions, and has sung the phrase "Lokah Samastha Sukhino Bhavantu" in 50 different languages. He is currently working on a detailed and scientific study of Vedas, Upanishads, Puranas, and the Bhagavad Gita. He has also composed and sung the Hanuman Chalisa and Gayatri Mantra in 108 and 1008 different compositions, respectively.

Awards - Four Times Guinness World Records, Winner of Mahatma Gandhi Vishwa Shanti Puraskar, Mahatma Gandhi Global Peace Ambassador, Kashi Ratna Award, Dr. APJ Abdul Kalam Motivational Person of the Year 2017, Mother Teresa Award, Indira Gandhi Priyadarshini Award, Bharat Vikas Ratna Award, Udyog Ratna Award, Vigyan Prasar Award, Poorvanchal Ratn Samman.

❧❧❧

Preface

The modern business landscape is constantly evolving, and to succeed in today's competitive environment, organizations must be strategic in their approach to business management. "Strategic Business Management: Navigating the Modern Business Landscape" is a comprehensive guide that explores the various aspects of strategic business management and provides practical insights and strategies for achieving business success.

The book covers a wide range of topics, including the external and internal business environment, competitive and corporate strategy, international business, business model innovation, organizational design and structure, leadership and decision-making, change management, operations management, supply chain management, project management, quality management, human resource management, marketing management, product management, brand management, pricing strategy, digital marketing, and sales management. Each chapter is written by experts in the field and provides in-depth analysis of the latest trends and best practices.

This book is designed for managers, entrepreneurs, and business students who are looking to gain a deeper understanding of strategic business management and learn how to navigate the modern business landscape. Whether you are just starting out in your career or are an experienced manager looking to improve your skills, this book will provide you with the knowledge and tools you need to succeed.

We hope that "Strategic Business Management: Navigating the Modern Business Landscape" will serve as a valuable resource for you as you navigate the ever-changing business world and achieve your business goals.

ϷϷϷ

ONE

Introduction to Strategic Business Management

1.1 The Importance of Strategic Business Management

Strategic business management is the process of making key decisions and taking action to ensure the long-term success of an organization. It involves setting goals, identifying opportunities, and allocating resources to achieve those goals. Strategic business management is essential for businesses of all sizes and industries as it helps them to navigate the rapidly changing business landscape and stay competitive.

1.2 The Role of Strategic Business Management in Today's Business Environment

The modern business environment is characterized by rapid change and increased competition. Globalization, digitalization, and advances in technology are all factors that have changed the way businesses operate. In order to stay competitive, organizations must be able to adapt to these changes and make strategic decisions that will drive their growth and success. Strategic business management is the key to doing so.

1.3 Key Elements of Strategic Business Management

Strategic business management involves several key elements, including:

Goal setting: Establishing long-term objectives for the organization

SWOT analysis: Identifying the organization's strengths, weaknesses, opportunities, and threats

Strategic planning: Developing a plan to achieve the organization's goals

Implementation: Taking action to implement the plan

Evaluation and control: Continuously monitoring and adjusting the plan as needed

1.4 Who Should Learn Strategic Business Management?

Strategic business management is essential for leaders and managers at all levels of an organization. Whether you are an entrepreneur, a manager, or an executive, understanding and applying the principles of strategic business management will help you to make better decisions and achieve your goals.

1.5 Conclusion

In this chapter, we have introduced the concept of strategic business management and discussed its importance in today's business environment. We have also outlined the key elements of strategic business management and highlighted the role it plays in helping organizations to navigate the rapidly changing business landscape and stay competitive. In the next chapter, we will delve deeper into the goal-setting and SWOT analysis components of strategic business management.

TWO

THE EXTERNAL BUSINESS ENVIRONMENT

2.1 Understanding the External Business Environment

The external business environment refers to the factors and forces outside of an organization that can impact its performance and decision-making. These can include economic, political, legal, technological, and societal factors. Understanding the external business environment is crucial for any organization as it can provide valuable information for making strategic decisions.

2.2 Economic Factors

Economic factors include things like interest rates, inflation, and unemployment rates. These factors can have a significant impact on an organization's bottom line, as they can affect consumer spending and the cost of goods and services. For example, a recession can lead to a decrease in consumer spending, which can negatively impact a business's sales and profits.

2.3 Political and Legal Factors

Political and legal factors refer to the actions and policies of government entities, as well as laws and regulations that govern business operations. These can include things like taxes, trade policies, and labor laws. Changes in political or legal factors can have a major impact on an organization, such as changes in tax laws which can affect the company's profitability.

2.4 Technological Factors

Technological factors refer to the advancements and innovations in technology that can impact an organization. These can include things like the development of new software, hardware, or communication technologies. Technological factors can also affect the way that businesses operate, such as the rise of e-commerce, which has changed the way that consumers shop and pay for goods and services.

2.5 Societal Factors

Societal factors refer to the cultural and demographic characteristics of a society. These can include things like population growth, age distribution, and income levels. Societal factors can affect an organization's marketing and sales strategies, as well as the types of products and services it offers. For example, an aging population may lead to increased demand for healthcare products and services.

2.6 Conclusion

In this chapter, we have discussed the external business environment and the various factors that can impact an organization. Understanding the external business environment is crucial for any organization as it can provide valuable information for making strategic decisions. In the next chapter, we will discuss the internal business environment and how it can be used to gain a competitive advantage.

ϷϷϷ

THREE

INTERNAL BUSINESS ANALYSIS

3.1 Understanding the Internal Business Environment

The internal business environment refers to the factors and forces within an organization that can impact its performance and decision-making. These can include organizational structure, resources, culture, and capabilities. Understanding the internal business environment is crucial for any organization as it can provide valuable information for making strategic decisions and identifying areas for improvement.

3.2 Organizational Structure

The organizational structure refers to the way that an organization is set up and how tasks and responsibilities are divided among different departments and individuals.

Different types of organizational structures include functional, divisional, matrix, and flat structures. The right organizational structure can help an organization to be more efficient and effective in achieving its goals.

3.3 Resources

Resources refer to the things that an organization has at its disposal, such as financial resources, human resources, and physical resources. These resources are necessary for an organization to operate and achieve its goals. Identifying and managing these resources effectively is crucial for any organization.

3.4 Culture

Culture refers to the shared values, beliefs, and practices within an organization. A positive organizational culture can lead to increased employee satisfaction, productivity, and commitment to the organization's goals. A negative organizational culture can lead to low morale, high turnover, and poor performance.

3.5 Capabilities

Capabilities refer to the skills, knowledge, and expertise of an organization's employees. These capabilities can give an organization a competitive advantage by enabling it to perform specific tasks or activities better than its competitors. Identifying and developing key capabilities within an organization can be a powerful tool for achieving strategic goals.

3.6 Conclusion

In this chapter, we have discussed the internal business environment and the various factors that can impact an organization. Understanding the internal business environment is crucial for any organization as it can provide valuable information for making strategic decisions and identifying areas for improvement. In the next chapter, we will discuss how to use internal and external analysis to make strategic decisions and achieve organizational goals.

ΡΡΡ

FOUR

Competitive Strategy

4.1 Understanding Competitive Strategy

Competitive strategy refers to the actions and decisions that an organization takes to gain a competitive advantage over its rivals. This can include things like differentiating products and services, creating barriers to entry, and leveraging internal strengths and resources. A well-crafted competitive strategy can help an organization to achieve long-term success in a highly competitive marketplace.

4.2 Generic Competitive Strategies

There are several generic competitive strategies that organizations can use to gain a competitive advantage. These include:

Cost leadership: This strategy involves reducing costs in order to offer products or services at a lower price than competitors.

Differentiation: This strategy involves offering unique or superior products or services that are valued by customers.

Focus: This strategy involves targeting a specific niche market or customer segment.

4.3 Porter's Five Forces Analysis

Porter's Five Forces Analysis is a framework used to analyze the competitive dynamics of an industry. It looks at five key factors: the threat of new entrants, the bargaining power of suppliers, the bargaining power of buyers, the threat of substitute products or services, and the intensity of competitive rivalry. By understanding these five forces, organizations can identify the key drivers of competition in their industry and develop strategies to gain a competitive advantage.

4.4 SWOT Analysis

SWOT Analysis is a framework used to analyze an organization's internal and external environment. It looks at four key factors: strengths, weaknesses, opportunities, and threats. By understanding these four factors, organizations can identify their key internal strengths and weaknesses as well as external opportunities and threats that they face. This can help organizations to develop strategies to leverage their strengths and opportunities, while mitigating their weaknesses and threats.

4.5 Conclusion

In this chapter, we have discussed competitive strategy and the various frameworks that organizations can use to gain a competitive advantage. By understanding the competitive dynamics of an industry and analyzing their internal and external environment, organizations can develop effective competitive strategies that can help them to achieve long-term success in a highly competitive marketplace. In the next chapter, we will discuss how organizations can implement their competitive strategy and achieve strategic goals.

ᐳᐳᐳ

FIVE

Corporate Strategy

5.1 Understanding Corporate Strategy

Corporate strategy refers to the actions and decisions that an organization takes to manage its portfolio of businesses and achieve its long-term goals. This can include things like diversifying into new markets or industries, making strategic acquisitions or divestitures, and managing risk. A well-crafted corporate strategy can help an organization to achieve sustainable growth and long-term success.

5.2 Corporate-level Strategies

There are several corporate-level strategies that organizations can use to manage their portfolio of businesses and achieve their long-term goals. These include:

Concentration: This strategy involves focusing on a specific business or product line.

Diversification: This strategy involves expanding into new markets or industries.

Integration: This strategy involves acquiring or merging with other companies to achieve economies of scale or scope.

5.3 Portfolio Analysis

Portfolio analysis is a framework used to evaluate an organization's portfolio of businesses and identify areas for improvement. One popular method for portfolio analysis is the Boston Consulting Group (BCG) matrix, which plots businesses on a grid based on their relative market share and growth potential. This can help organizations to identify which businesses to invest in and which businesses to divest.

5.4 Managing Risk

Corporate strategy also involves managing risk. This can include identifying potential risks and developing contingency plans, as well as implementing risk management processes and procedures. Organizations can use various tools and techniques to manage risk, such as scenario planning and risk assessments.

5.5 Conclusion

In this chapter, we have discussed corporate strategy and the various frameworks and techniques that organizations can use to manage their portfolio of businesses and achieve their long-term goals. By evaluating their portfolio of businesses, identifying areas for improvement and managing risk, organizations can develop effective corporate strategies that can help them to achieve sustainable growth and long-term success. In the next chapter, we will discuss how organizations can implement their corporate strategy and achieve strategic goals.

ԾԾԾ

SIX

INTERNATIONAL BUSINESS STRATEGY

6.1 Understanding International Business Strategy

International business strategy refers to the actions and decisions that an organization takes to compete effectively in global markets. This can include things like entering new international markets, adapting products and services to meet local needs, and managing cross-cultural differences. A well-crafted international business strategy can help an organization to achieve global expansion and long-term success.

6.2 Entry Strategies

There are several entry strategies that organizations can use to enter international markets, including:

Exporting: This strategy involves selling products or services to customers in other countries.

Licensing: This strategy involves allowing a foreign company to use an organization's technology or intellectual property in exchange for royalties or fees.

Franchising: This strategy involves allowing a foreign company to operate an organization's business model in exchange for royalties or fees.

Joint ventures: This strategy involves forming a partnership with a foreign company to enter a new market.

Wholly-owned subsidiaries: This strategy involves creating a new company in a foreign market that is owned and controlled by the organization.

6.3 Adapting to Local Markets

Adapting to local markets is an important aspect of international business strategy. Organizations need to understand the cultural, economic, and legal differences in each country they operate in and adapt their products, services, and business practices accordingly. This can include things like localizing products and services, building relationships with local partners, and complying with local regulations.

6.4 Managing Cultural Differences

Managing cultural differences is also an important aspect of international business strategy. Organizations need to understand and appreciate the cultural differences in each country they operate in and develop effective communication and management strategies to navigate these differences. This can include things like cross-cultural training, building diverse teams, and developing global management skills.

6.5 Conclusion

In this chapter, we have discussed international business strategy and the various entry strategies, adaptation strategies, and cultural management strategies that organizations can use to compete effectively in global markets. By understanding the cultural, economic, and legal differences in each country they operate in, and adapting their products, services, and business practices accordingly, organizations can develop effective international business strategies that can help them to achieve global expansion and long-term success. In the next chapter, we will discuss how organizations can implement their international business strategy and achieve strategic goals.

⮞⮞⮞

SEVEN

BUSINESS MODEL INNOVATION

7.1 Understanding Business Model Innovation

Business model innovation refers to the process of creating and implementing new or significantly improved ways of doing business. It involves rethinking how an organization creates, delivers, and captures value for its customers and stakeholders. Business model innovation can help organizations to stay competitive, enter new markets, and achieve long-term success.

7.2 Types of Business Model Innovation

There are several types of business model innovation, including:

Incremental: This type of innovation involves making small changes to an existing business model to improve efficiency or customer value.

Radical: This type of innovation involves creating a completely new business model that disrupts existing markets or creates new ones.

Platform-based: This type of innovation involves creating a digital platform that connects customers, partners, and other stakeholders to create new value.

Business model design: This type of innovation involves taking a systematic approach to designing a business model to achieve specific goals.

7.3 The Business Model Canvas

The business model canvas is a visual tool that can help organizations to map out and design their business models. It is a simple and flexible tool that can be used to identify key components of a business model, such as customer segments, value propositions, revenue streams, and key resources.

7.4 Business Model Innovation Process

Business model innovation is not a one-time event, but rather a continuous process that involves testing and refining new ideas. The process can be broken down into several stages:

Idea generation: This stage involves generating new ideas for business models.

Conceptualization: This stage involves taking a new idea and turning it into a concrete concept.

Prototyping: This stage involves creating a minimal viable product (MVP) to test the concept with customers.

Implementation: This stage involves scaling the business model and making it a part of the organization's operations.

7.5 Conclusion

In this chapter, we have discussed business model innovation and the various types of innovation, tools, and processes that organizations can use to create and implement new or significantly improved ways of doing business. By rethinking how they create, deliver, and capture value for their customers and stakeholders, organizations can develop effective business models that can help them to stay competitive, enter new markets, and achieve long-term success. In the next chapter, we will discuss how organizations can implement their business model innovation and achieve strategic goals.

ÞÞÞ

EIGHT

ORGANIZATIONAL DESIGN AND STRUCTURE

8.1 Understanding Organizational Design and Structure

Organizational design and structure refers to the way an organization is set up to achieve its goals. It involves making decisions about how work will be divided, how tasks will be coordinated, how information will flow, and how power will be distributed. The right organizational design and structure can help organizations to be more efficient, responsive, and effective.

8.2 Types of Organizational Design and Structure

There are several types of organizational design and structure, including:

Functional: This type of structure groups employees by

their area of expertise, such as marketing, finance, or human resources.

Divisional: This type of structure groups employees by product, service, or geographic area.

Matrix: This type of structure combines elements of functional and divisional structures, creating cross-functional teams to work on specific projects or product lines.

Network: This type of structure involves creating partnerships and alliances with other organizations to achieve common goals.

Flat: This type of structure is characterized by a minimal hierarchy, with a small number of layers between the top executives and the front-line employees.

8.3 Organizational Design Process

Organizational design is not a one-time event, but rather a continuous process that involves adjusting the structure and design of an organization to better align with its goals and objectives. The process can be broken down into several stages:

Analysis: This stage involves analyzing the current organizational design and structure to identify any gaps or inefficiencies.

Design: This stage involves creating a new design and structure that aligns with the organization's goals and objectives.

Implementation: This stage involves putting the new design and structure in place, including making any necessary changes to roles, responsibilities, and processes.

Evaluation: This stage involves evaluating the effectiveness of the new design and structure, making any necessary adjustments, and monitoring progress.

8.4 Conclusion

In this chapter, we have discussed organizational design and structure and the various types of structures and processes that organizations can use to set up their organization to achieve their goals. By making the right decisions about how work will be divided, how tasks will be coordinated, how information will flow, and how power will be distributed, organizations can develop effective organizational design and structure that can help them to be more efficient, responsive, and effective. In the next chapter, we will discuss how organizations can implement their organizational design and structure and achieve strategic goals.

NINE

Leadership and Decision Making

9.1 Understanding Leadership and Decision Making

Leadership and decision making are closely related concepts in the field of strategic business management. Leadership refers to the ability to influence and guide others to achieve a common goal. Decision making refers to the process of choosing among alternative courses of action. Effective leaders must not only be able to make good decisions, but also be able to inspire and motivate others to follow through on those decisions.

9.2 Types of Leadership

There are several types of leadership, including:

Autocratic: This type of leadership involves one person

making all the decisions, without input from others.

Democratic: This type of leadership involves involving others in the decision-making process, through techniques such as consensus building and voting.

Transformational: This type of leadership involves inspiring and motivating others to achieve a shared vision or goal.

Servant: This type of leadership involves putting the needs of others before one's own, and working to empower and develop others.

9.3 Decision Making Process

The decision making process can be broken down into several stages, including:

Problem Identification: This stage involves identifying the problem or decision that needs to be made.

Information Gathering: This stage involves gathering and analyzing information related to the problem or decision.

Alternatives Generation: This stage involves generating a list of potential alternatives or solutions.

Alternatives Evaluation: This stage involves evaluating the potential alternatives or solutions based on their pros and cons and their alignment with the organization's goals and objectives.

Decision Implementation: This stage involves putting the chosen solution into action.

Decision Evaluation: This stage involves evaluating the effectiveness of the decision and making any necessary adjustments.

9.4 Conclusion

In this chapter, we have discussed the concepts of leadership and decision making and how they are closely related to each other. We also discussed various types of leadership styles and the decision-making process. Effective leadership is not just about making the right decisions, but also about inspiring and motivating others to follow through on those decisions. Effective decision making is not just about solving a problem, but also about making sure that the solution is aligned with the organization's goals and objectives. In the next chapter, we will discuss how organizations can implement effective change management strategies to achieve strategic goals.

ﭖﭖﭖ

TEN

CHANGE MANAGEMENT

10.1 Introduction

Change management is a critical aspect of strategic business management as organizations must continuously adapt to the ever-changing business landscape. Change management involves planning, implementing, and monitoring changes within an organization in order to achieve strategic goals and objectives. It also involves effectively communicating and managing the impact of the change on employees, customers, and other stakeholders.

10.2 The Change Management Process

The change management process can be broken down into several stages, including:

Assessment: This stage involves identifying the need for change and assessing the current state of the organization.

Planning: This stage involves developing a plan for the change, including identifying specific goals and objectives, timelines, and resources needed.

Implementation: This stage involves putting the plan into action, including communicating the change to stakeholders and training employees on any new processes or procedures.

Monitoring: This stage involves monitoring the progress of the change and making any necessary adjustments.

Evaluation: This stage involves evaluating the effectiveness of the change and making any necessary improvements for future changes.

10.3 Communicating Change

Effective communication is crucial for successful change management. It is important to communicate the change clearly and transparently to all stakeholders, including employees, customers, and other stakeholders. This can be done through a variety of methods, such as meetings, town halls, newsletters, and social media. It is also important to address any concerns or resistance to the change and provide support for employees during the transition.

10.4 Managing Resistance to Change

Resistance to change is a natural reaction and should be anticipated and managed effectively. Some common reasons for resistance include fear of the unknown, lack of understanding, and loss of control. To manage resistance, it is important to involve employees in the change process, provide training and support, and communicate the benefits of the change.

10.5 Conclusion

In this chapter, we have discussed the importance of change management in strategic business management. We have also discussed the change management process and key considerations for effective communication and managing resistance to change. Change is inevitable in today's business landscape and organizations must be able to effectively manage change in order to achieve strategic goals and objectives. In the next chapter, we will discuss the importance of effective risk management in achieving organizational goals.

ᗡᗡᗡ

ELEVEN

OPERATIONS MANAGEMENT

11.1 Introduction

Operations management is a critical aspect of strategic business management as it deals with the planning, coordination, and control of the activities that transform inputs into finished goods and services. The goal of operations management is to efficiently and effectively use resources to produce goods and services that meet the needs of customers.

11.2 The Operations Management Process

The operations management process can be broken down into several stages, including:

Design: This stage involves designing the processes and systems that will be used to produce goods and services. This includes determining the most efficient layout of facilities, equipment, and personnel.

Planning: This stage involves creating a plan for how resources will be used to produce goods and services. This includes determining the quantities of raw materials and other inputs that will be needed, as well as scheduling production.

Execution: This stage involves putting the plan into action, including coordinating the activities of personnel, equipment, and materials.

Monitoring and Control: This stage involves monitoring the performance of the operations, including tracking production metrics such as output, quality, and efficiency. Any issues or deviations from the plan are identified and addressed in this stage.

Continual Improvement: This stage involves continuously improving the operations by identifying areas for improvement, implementing changes, and evaluating the effectiveness of those changes.

11.3 Lean Operations

Lean operations is a methodology for improving efficiency and effectiveness in operations management. It is based on the principles of eliminating waste, maximizing value for customers, and continuously improving processes. Key practices in lean operations include:

Value Stream Mapping: This is a process of identifying and analyzing the flow of materials and information in a process, with the goal of identifying areas of waste and inefficiency.

Kaizen: This is a practice of continuous improvement, where employees at all levels are encouraged to identify and implement improvements in processes.

Just-in-time (JIT) inventory: This is a practice of producing and delivering goods and services as they are needed, rather than producing and storing large quantities of inventory.

11.4 Conclusion

In this chapter, we have discussed the importance of operations management in strategic business management. We have also discussed the operations management process and key practices for improving efficiency and effectiveness, such as lean operations. Effective operations management is essential for producing goods and services that meet the needs of customers and for achieving strategic goals and objectives. In the next chapter, we will discuss the importance of supply chain management in achieving organizational goals.

ᐁᐁᐁ

TWELVE

SUPPLY CHAIN MANAGEMENT

12.1 Introduction

Supply chain management is the coordination and management of all activities involved in sourcing, procurement, conversion, and logistics management. It encompasses the entire flow of materials, information, and finances from suppliers to customers. Effective supply chain management is critical to achieving organizational goals and objectives, as it can have a significant impact on cost, quality, and delivery performance.

12.2 Supply Chain Strategy

A key element of supply chain management is the development of a supply chain strategy. This includes determining the optimal mix of suppliers, logistics partners, and inventory levels to meet organizational goals and objectives. Factors to consider in developing a supply chain strategy include:

Cost: The cost of goods and services, including the cost of raw materials, transportation, and logistics.

Quality: The quality of goods and services, including product and service quality as well as supplier quality.

Delivery Performance: The ability to meet customer demand for goods and services, including lead times and delivery schedules.

Flexibility: The ability to respond quickly to changes in demand or supply.

Risk Management: Identifying and managing potential risks in the supply chain, such as disruptions in the supply of raw materials or changes in demand.

12.3 Supply Chain Planning and Control

Effective supply chain planning and control is essential for achieving organizational goals and objectives. This includes:

Sales and Operations Planning (S&OP): The process of aligning demand and supply, including setting production and inventory levels to meet customer demand.

Inventory Management: The process of managing inventory levels, including determining optimal inventory levels and managing inventory turnover.

Transportation and Logistics Management: The process of

managing the movement of goods, including determining the most cost-effective and efficient methods of transportation and logistics.

12.4 Supply Chain Collaboration and Partnership

Collaboration and partnership with suppliers, logistics partners, and other supply chain partners can lead to significant improvements in cost, quality, and delivery performance. Key practices in supply chain collaboration and partnership include:

Supplier Relationship Management: Managing the relationship with suppliers to ensure they are meeting organizational goals and objectives.

Collaborative Planning, Forecasting, and Replenishment (CPFR): Collaborating with suppliers and customers to align demand and supply.

Supply Chain Visibility: Sharing information with suppliers and logistics partners to improve coordination and decision-making.

12.5 Conclusion

In this chapter, we have discussed the importance of supply chain management in achieving organizational goals and objectives. We have also discussed key elements of supply chain management, including supply chain strategy, planning and control, and collaboration and partnership. Effective supply chain management is essential for achieving strategic goals and objectives, and for ensuring that goods and services are delivered to customers in a timely and cost-effective manner. In the next chapter, we will discuss the importance of information technology in achieving strategic goals and objectives.

ᏘᏘᏘ

THIRTEEN

Project Management

13.1 Introduction

Project management is the process of planning, organizing, and managing resources to achieve specific goals and objectives. It is a critical aspect of business management, as it allows organizations to plan and execute projects effectively, in order to achieve their strategic goals and objectives.

13.2 Project Planning

Project planning is the process of defining the project goals and objectives, and determining the resources required to achieve them. This includes:

Defining the project scope: Identifying what the project will achieve and what it will not achieve.

Developing a project schedule: Identifying the tasks that

need to be completed and the order in which they will be completed.

Estimating project costs: Determining the financial resources required to complete the project.

Identifying project risks: Identifying potential problems that may occur during the project and developing strategies to mitigate them.

13.3 Project Execution

Project execution is the process of carrying out the project according to the plan. This includes:

Managing project resources: Ensuring that the resources required to complete the project are available and being used effectively.

Monitoring project progress: Tracking the progress of the project and making adjustments as needed.

Communicating with stakeholders: Keeping stakeholders informed of project progress and addressing any concerns they may have.

13.4 Project Control

Project control is the process of monitoring and managing the project to ensure that it stays on track and is completed on time and within budget. This includes:

Monitoring project performance: Tracking the progress of the project and comparing it to the plan.

Making adjustments as needed: Making changes to the project plan as necessary to keep the project on track.

Managing project risks: Identifying and managing potential problems that may occur during the project.

13.5 Project Closure

Project closure is the final phase of the project management process, and includes:

Completing the project: Ensuring that all project tasks are completed and that the project goals and objectives have been achieved.

Conducting a project review: Reviewing the project to identify areas for improvement and to make recommendations for future projects.

Documenting project results: Recording the project results for future reference.

13.6 Conclusion

In this chapter, we have discussed the importance of project management in achieving organizational goals and objectives. We have also discussed key elements of project management, including project planning, execution, control, and closure. Effective project management is essential for ensuring that projects are completed on time, within budget, and to the satisfaction of stakeholders. In the next chapter, we will discuss the importance of performance management in achieving strategic goals and objectives.

❧❧❧

FOURTEEN

QUALITY MANAGEMENT

14.1 Introduction

Quality management is the process of ensuring that products and services meet or exceed customer expectations. It is a critical aspect of business management, as it allows organizations to improve their competitiveness, increase customer satisfaction, and reduce costs.

14.2 Total Quality Management (TQM)

Total Quality Management (TQM) is a management philosophy that focuses on continuous improvement of products and services through the involvement of all employees. It includes:

Establishing customer-focused goals and objectives

Involving all employees in the quality improvement process

Continuously monitoring and measuring performance

Making data-driven decisions

Continuously improving products, services, and processes

14.3 Quality Control

Quality control is the process of inspecting and testing products and services to ensure that they meet or exceed customer expectations. It includes:

Establishing quality standards: Defining the level of quality that products and services should meet.

Inspecting and testing products and services: Checking products and services to ensure that they meet the established quality standards.

Identifying and addressing quality issues: Finding and correcting any problems that do not meet quality standards.

14.4 Quality Assurance

Quality assurance is the process of ensuring that products and services meet or exceed customer expectations by preventing quality issues from occurring. It includes:

Developing and implementing quality management systems: Creating procedures and processes to ensure that quality standards are met.

Providing training and resources: Providing employees with the necessary training and resources to meet quality standards.

Continuously monitoring and measuring performance: Continuously checking products and services to ensure that they meet quality standards.

14.5 Continuous Improvement

Continuous improvement is the ongoing process of identifying opportunities for improvement and making changes to products, services, and processes to increase quality and efficiency. It includes:

Gathering and analyzing data: Collecting data on products, services, and processes to identify areas for improvement.

Implementing changes: Making changes to products, services, and processes based on data analysis.

Monitoring the results: Continuously monitoring the results of changes to ensure that they have the desired effect.

14.6 Conclusion

In this chapter, we have discussed the importance of quality management in achieving organizational goals and objectives. We have also discussed key elements of quality management, including Total Quality Management (TQM), Quality Control, Quality Assurance, and Continuous Improvement. Effective quality management is essential for ensuring that products and services meet or exceed customer expectations and for improving the competitiveness of the organization. In the next chapter, we will discuss the importance of customer relationship management in achieving strategic goals and objectives.

ᐅᐅᐅ

FIFTEEN

Human Resource Management

15.1 Introduction

Human Resource Management (HRM) is the process of managing and developing an organization's human capital, which includes recruiting, hiring, training, managing, and developing employees. It is a critical aspect of business management, as it allows organizations to attract and retain top talent, improve employee performance, and build a positive organizational culture.

15.2 Recruitment and Selection

Recruitment and selection is the process of identifying and attracting candidates for open positions within an organization. It includes:

Identifying staffing needs: Determining the number and types of positions that need to be filled.

Developing job descriptions and specifications: Defining the duties, responsibilities, and qualifications required for open positions.

Attracting candidates: Advertising open positions and actively recruiting candidates.

Screening and selecting candidates: Reviewing resumes, conducting interviews, and selecting the most qualified candidates.

15.3 Training and Development

Training and development is the process of providing employees with the knowledge, skills, and abilities they need to perform their jobs effectively. It includes:

Identifying training needs: Determining the specific training needs of employees based on job performance and organizational goals.

Developing training programs: Creating training programs that address identified needs.

Delivering training: Providing employees with the training they need.

Assessing the effectiveness of training: Evaluating the effectiveness of training programs to ensure that they are meeting their intended goals.

15.4 Performance Management

Performance management is the process of setting goals, evaluating employee performance, and providing feedback to improve performance. It includes:

Setting goals: Defining what an employee should achieve in their role.

Monitoring performance: Tracking and measuring employee performance against set goals.

Providing feedback: Communicating feedback to employees on their performance.

Recognizing and rewarding good performance: Providing recognition and rewards for meeting or exceeding goals.

15.5 Employee Relations

Employee relations is the process of managing the relationships between employees and management. It includes:

Communicating with employees: Regularly communicating with employees to ensure that they are informed and engaged.

Addressing employee concerns: Resolving employee concerns and complaints.

Managing employee engagement: Building a positive

organizational culture and keeping employees engaged.

15.6 Conclusion

In this chapter, we have discussed the importance of Human Resource Management in achieving organizational goals and objectives. We have also discussed key elements of HRM, including Recruitment and Selection, Training and Development, Performance Management, and Employee Relations. Effective HRM is essential for attracting and retaining top talent, improving employee performance, and building a positive organizational culture. In the next chapter, we will discuss the importance of financial management in achieving strategic goals and objectives.

ᐅᐅᐅ

SIXTEEN
MARKETING MANAGEMENT

16.1 Introduction

Marketing management is the process of planning, implementing, and controlling the marketing efforts of an organization. It involves identifying the target market, developing a marketing mix (product, price, place, and promotion), and managing the marketing budget. Effective marketing management is essential for creating and maintaining a sustainable competitive advantage, building brand awareness, and increasing revenue.

16.2 Target Market

The target market is the specific group of consumers that an organization aims to reach with its marketing efforts. Identifying the target market involves analyzing the demographics, psychographics, and behaviors of potential customers. This information is used to develop a marketing strategy that addresses the specific needs and wants of the target market.

16.3 Marketing Mix

The marketing mix is the combination of product, price, place, and promotion used to reach the target market.

Product: The product or service offered to the target market.

Price: The price at which the product or service is sold.

Place: The location where the product or service is sold.

Promotion: The methods used to communicate the product or service to the target market.

16.4 Marketing Budget

The marketing budget is the amount of money allocated for marketing efforts. It includes the costs of research, product development, advertising, promotions, and distribution. The marketing budget must be managed effectively to ensure that resources are allocated in a way that maximizes return on investment.

16.5 Marketing Research

Marketing research is the process of gathering, analyzing, and interpreting information about the target market and the marketing environment. It is used to inform the development of the marketing strategy and to make data-driven decisions about the marketing mix.

16.6 Branding and Brand Management

Branding is the process of creating a unique name and image for a product or service in the minds of consumers. Brand management is the process of maintaining and building the brand through consistent messaging and communication. A strong brand can create customer loyalty and increase the value of the organization.

16.7 Conclusion

In this chapter, we have discussed the importance of marketing management in achieving organizational goals and objectives. We have also discussed key elements of marketing management, including target market, marketing mix, marketing budget, marketing research, branding and brand management. Effective marketing management is essential for creating and maintaining a sustainable competitive advantage, building brand awareness, and increasing revenue. In the next chapter, we will discuss the role of information technology in strategic business management.

SEVENTEEN

PRODUCT MANAGEMENT

17.1 Introduction

Product management is the process of developing and managing a product throughout its lifecycle, from idea generation to end-of-life. It involves conducting market research, identifying customer needs and wants, developing a product strategy, and overseeing the design, development, and launch of the product. Effective product management is essential for creating and delivering products that meet customer needs and drive revenue growth.

17.2 Product Lifecycle

A product goes through various stages throughout its lifecycle, including development, introduction, growth, maturity, and decline. Product managers must understand the stage of the product lifecycle and develop strategies to manage the product accordingly.

Development: This stage is where the product idea is generated and the product is developed.

Introduction: This stage is where the product is launched and introduced to the market.

Growth: This stage is where the product starts to gain acceptance and sales begin to increase.

Maturity: This stage is where the product reaches its peak sales and starts to plateau.

Decline: This stage is where the product sales start to decline and eventually the product is phased out.

17.3 Market Research

Market research is an essential aspect of product management. It involves gathering and analyzing information about the target market, competitors, and industry trends. Market research is used to identify customer needs and wants, and to inform the development of the product strategy.

17.4 Product Strategy

Product strategy is the plan for the product, including its positioning, pricing, and promotion. It includes the target market, the unique selling proposition, and the product's competitive advantage. The product strategy should align with the overall organizational strategy.

17.5 Product Development

Product development involves the design, engineering, and testing of the product. It is a critical aspect of product management, as it ensures that the product meets the needs of the target market and is of high quality.

17.6 Product Launch

Product launch is the process of introducing the product to the market. It includes the development of a launch plan, which includes the timing, budget, and promotion of the product. A successful product launch can lead to increased revenue and market share.

17.7 Conclusion

In this chapter, we have discussed the importance of product management in achieving organizational goals and objectives. We have also discussed key elements of product management, including product lifecycle, market research, product strategy, product development, and product launch. Effective product management is essential for creating and delivering products that meet customer needs and drive revenue growth. In the next chapter, we will discuss the role of supply chain management in strategic business management.

ᗡᗡᗡ

EIGHTEEN

BRAND MANAGEMENT

18.1 Introduction

Brand management is the process of creating, developing, and maintaining a brand. A brand is the set of perceptions, emotions, and associations that a consumer has about a product or service. A strong brand can differentiate a product or service from competitors, create customer loyalty, and drive revenue growth.

18.2 Brand Identity

Brand identity is the visual and verbal elements that make up a brand. It includes the brand name, logo, color scheme, and messaging. A strong brand identity can help to create brand recognition and differentiate a product or service from competitors.

18.3 Brand Positioning

Brand positioning is the process of creating a unique image for a brand in the mind of the consumer. It involves identifying the target market and the benefits that the brand offers to that market. A strong brand positioning can help to create brand recognition and differentiate a product or service from competitors.

18.4 Brand Equity

Brand equity is the value that a brand adds to a product or service. It is the difference between the price that a consumer is willing to pay for a product or service with a brand and the price they would be willing to pay for the same product or service without a brand. A strong brand equity can drive revenue growth.

18.5 Brand Management Process

The brand management process includes the following steps:

Brand research: This step involves gathering information about the target market and the competition.

Brand strategy development: This step involves developing a brand strategy that aligns with the overall organizational strategy.

Brand implementation: This step involves implementing the brand strategy and creating brand identity elements.

Brand monitoring: This step involves monitoring the brand's performance and making adjustments as necessary.

18.6 Brand Crisis Management

Brand crisis management is the process of dealing with negative events that can damage a brand's reputation. It involves identifying potential crisis situations, developing a crisis management plan, and executing that plan in the event of a crisis.

18.7 Conclusion

In this chapter, we have discussed the importance of brand management in achieving organizational goals and objectives. We have also discussed key elements of brand management, including brand identity, brand positioning, brand equity, and the brand management process. Strong brand management can differentiate a product or service from competitors, create customer loyalty, and drive revenue growth. In the next chapter, we will discuss the importance of human resource management in strategic business management.

ᐳᐳᐳ

NINETEEN
PRICING STRATEGY

19.1 Introduction

Pricing strategy is the process of determining the price at which a product or service will be sold. The price of a product or service can have a significant impact on its success in the marketplace, and as such, pricing strategy is an important aspect of strategic business management.

19.2 Factors Affecting Pricing

There are several factors that can affect pricing strategy, including:

Cost of production: The cost of producing a product or delivering a service will have a direct impact on the price that can be charged.

Target market: The target market for a product or service will affect the price that can be charged. For example, products or services targeting premium markets can command higher prices than those targeting budget markets.

Competition: The price of similar products or services offered by competitors will affect the price that can be charged.

Distribution channels: The channels through which a product or service is distributed will affect the price that can be charged.

19.3 Pricing Methods

There are several pricing methods that can be used to determine the price of a product or service, including:

Cost-plus pricing: This method involves adding a markup to the cost of production to determine the price.

Value-based pricing: This method involves determining the price based on the perceived value of the product or service to the customer.

Penetration pricing: This method involves setting a low price initially to penetrate the market and gain market share.

Skimming pricing: This method involves setting a high price initially and gradually decreasing it over time.

19.4 Pricing Strategies

There are several pricing strategies that can be used, including:

Premium pricing: This strategy involves setting a high price for a product or service to convey its exclusivity or superior quality.

Economy pricing: This strategy involves setting a low price for a product or service to appeal to budget-conscious consumers.

Psychological pricing: This strategy involves setting a price that creates a certain perception or emotion in the customer.

19.5 Conclusion

In this chapter, we have discussed the importance of pricing strategy in strategic business management. We have also discussed key factors that can affect pricing and different pricing methods and strategies that can be used. An effective pricing strategy can help to maximize revenue and achieve organizational goals and objectives. In the next chapter, we will discuss the importance of marketing management in strategic business management.

ppp

TWENTY

DIGITAL MARKETING

20.1 Introduction

Digital marketing is the use of digital channels, such as the internet, social media, email, and mobile apps, to promote products or services. Digital marketing has become increasingly important as more and more consumers use digital channels to research and purchase products and services.

20.2 Key Digital Marketing Channels

There are several key digital marketing channels that can be used to reach consumers, including:

Website: A company's website is often the first point of contact for consumers and can be used to provide information about products or services, as well as to generate leads or make sales.

Search engine optimization (SEO): SEO is the process of optimizing a website to rank higher in search engine results. This can help to increase visibility and drive more traffic to a website.

Search engine marketing (SEM): SEM is the process of using paid advertising to appear at the top of search engine results.

Social media: Social media platforms, such as Facebook, Instagram, and Twitter, can be used to engage with consumers and promote products or services.

Email marketing: Email marketing is the process of sending marketing messages to a list of subscribers.

Mobile marketing: Mobile marketing is the process of reaching consumers through mobile devices, such as smartphones and tablets.

20.3 Digital Marketing Strategies

There are several digital marketing strategies that can be used to reach consumers, including:

Content marketing: This strategy involves creating valuable and relevant content to attract and engage consumers.

Influencer marketing: This strategy involves partnering with individuals or organizations who have a large following on social media to promote products or services.

Affiliate marketing: This strategy involves partnering with other companies or individuals to promote products or services in exchange for a commission.

Retargeting: This strategy involves using cookies or other technologies to show targeted ads to consumers who have previously visited a website.

20.4 Measuring and Analyzing Digital Marketing Efforts

It is important to measure and analyze the effectiveness of digital marketing efforts. Metrics such as website traffic, conversion rates, and social media engagement can be used to evaluate the success of digital marketing campaigns.

20.5 Conclusion

In this chapter, we have discussed the importance of digital marketing in strategic business management. We have also discussed key digital marketing channels and strategies that can be used to reach consumers. An effective digital marketing strategy can help to increase visibility and drive more traffic to a website, which can help to generate leads and make sales. In the next chapter, we will discuss how to effectively manage a brand in today's digital age.

ppp

TWENTY-ONE

SALES MANAGEMENT

21.1 Introduction

Sales management is the process of planning, organizing, and controlling the activities of a sales team. Sales management is an essential part of strategic business management as it is responsible for generating revenue for the organization.

21.2 Sales Planning

Sales planning involves setting sales goals and objectives, developing a sales strategy, and creating a sales forecast. The sales plan should align with the overall business strategy and should be reviewed and updated regularly.

21.3 Sales Organizing

Sales organizing involves structuring the sales team, including determining the number of salespeople needed and their roles and responsibilities. It also involves creating a sales territory, setting sales quotas, and establishing sales processes and procedures.

21.4 Sales Controlling

Sales controlling involves monitoring and evaluating the performance of the sales team. This includes setting sales targets, measuring sales performance, and providing feedback and coaching to the sales team. Sales controlling also involves making adjustments to the sales plan and strategy as needed.

21.5 Sales Techniques

There are several sales techniques that can be used to increase sales, including:

Solution selling: This technique focuses on understanding the customer's needs and providing a solution that meets those needs.

Consultative selling: This technique involves building a relationship with the customer and acting as a consultant to help them make informed decisions.

Relationship selling: This technique involves building long-term relationships with customers to increase sales over time.

21.6 Sales Technology

Technology can be used to improve the efficiency and

effectiveness of the sales process. This includes customer relationship management (CRM) software, which can be used to track and manage customer interactions, and sales automation software, which can be used to automate repetitive tasks and provide real-time sales data.

21.7 Conclusion

In this chapter, we have discussed the importance of sales management in strategic business management. Sales management is responsible for generating revenue for the organization and plays a key role in achieving the overall business strategy. Effective sales management involves planning, organizing, and controlling the activities of the sales team, as well as utilizing various sales techniques and technology to improve performance. In the next chapter, we will discuss how to effectively manage a company's financial resources.

ᐁᐁᐁ

TWENTY-TWO

FINANCIAL MANAGEMENT

Other Books Of The Author

1. The Moments When I Met God
2. Kashiyile Theertha Pathangal
3. GURU GYAN VANI
4. Abhiprerak Gita
5. ASSI SE JAIN GHAT TAK
6. Hopelessness of Arjuna
7. The Soul and It's True Nature
8. Sense of Action (Karma)
9. Action through Wisdom
10. Action through Wisdom
11. THEORY AND PRACTICAL OF EVERY ACTION
12. LOGICAL UNDERSTANDING OF THE SUPREME
13. THE IMPERISHABLE SUPREME
14. Yatra Nishadraj se Hanuman Ghat Tak
15. Yatra Karnatak Ghat se Raja Ghat Tak
16. Yatra Pandey Ghat se Prayagraj Ghat Tak
17. Yatra Ranjendra Prasad Ghat se Dattatreya Ghat Tak
18. YaatraSindhiya Ghat se Gwaliar Ghat Tak
19. Yatra Mangala Gauri Ghat se Hanuman Gadhi Ghat Tak
20. Yatra Gaay Ghat Se Nishad Ghat Tak
21. MAA GANGA, GHATEN EVM UTSAV
22. Ganga Arti Dev Deepavali evam Any Utsav
23. Potentials of Digitalized India
24. VEDIC CONSCIOUSNESS
25. A Brief Introduction to Vedic Science
26. Kashi ke Barah Jyotirling
27. IMPACT OF MOTIVATION
28. Let's have a Milky Way Journey
29. Color Therapy in a Nutshell

30. Rigveda in a Nutshell
31. Yajurveda in a Nutshell
32. Samveda in a Nutshell
33. Atharva Veda in a Nutshell
34. Ayushman Bhava - Ayurveda
35. Srimad Bhagavad Gita and Upanishad Connection
36. Srimad Bhagavad Gita - an attempt to summarize each chapter.
37. Facts and Impact of Nakshatra
38. Astro Gems - NAVARATNA
39. Ekadashi - A Concise Overview
40. A Concise View of Hanuman Chalisa
41. Inspirational Gita
42. Nakshatraranyam
43. Summary of 18 Mahapuranas
44. Synopsis of 18 Upa Puranas
45. Rigvediya Upanishads
46. Shukla Yajurvediya Upanishads
47. Krishna Yajurvediya Upanishads
48. Samavediya Upanishads
49. Atharvavediya Upanishads
50. The Seven Great Sages
51. From Rocket Scientist to President Dr. APJ Abdul Kalam
52. The Visionary's Voice - Quotes of Dr. APJ Abdul Kalam
53. The Wisdom of Swami Vivekananda: Insights and Inspiration from a Legendary Spiritual Teacher
54. Ayurvedic Remedies from the Garden
55. Sages and Seers
56. Rising Strong – Motivational Stories of Women
57. Beyond Flames -Mystery stories of Funeral Ghat Manikarnika
58. The Origins of Tulsi: A Look at the Mythological Roots of the Plant"

59. The Holistic Cow: A Look at the Physical, Spiritual, and Cultural Importance of Cows in India
60. Arts of Healing
61. Exploring the Divine
62. Understanding Five Elements
63. The Etymology of Ram
64. Symbols of India
65. Voice of Change (About Speeches of Great Men)
66. She Speaks (About Speeches of Great Women)
67. Patriotism on Celluloid – Brief About Patriotic Films
68. The Music of Motivation: A Brief Guide to Inspirational Film Songs
69. **Unlocking the Secrets of the Dashopanishads**
70. A Cultural Mosaic
71. Ancient Traditions, Modern Minds
72. Ecos of Ancient Wisdom
73. Beneath the Surface
74. From Temples to Ashrams
75. Sages of the Subcontinent
76. The Art of Healling (Ayurveda, Yoga & Naturopathy)
77. Indian Kitchen
78. The Festivals of India
79. The Indian Epics Retold
80. The Power of Mantras
81. The Indian River Ganges
82. The Indian Architecture
83. Rites of Passage
84. The Indian Silk Road
85. The Indian Literature
86. The Indian Villages
87. The Indian Folks & Crafts
88. The Way of Buddha
89. The Ramayan of Tulsidas

ppp

Contact

DR. JAGADEESH PILLAI

MBA & PhD in Vedic Science

Four Times Guinness World Record Holder

Winner of Mahatma Gandhi Vishwa Shanti Puraskar and
Global Peace Ambassador

Gemology, Astro & Vastu Consultant - Spiritual Counselor

Consultant for designing World Record Ideas

Efficient Tarot Card Reader

9839093003

myrichindia@gmail.com

drjagadeeshpillai@facebook

drjagadeeshpillai@instagram
jagadeeshpillai@youtube

www. JAGADEESHPILLAI.com

ॐॐॐ

|| LOKAHA SAMASTHAHA SUKHINO BHAVANTU ||

❧ ❧ ❧